W9-BYH-957

Cloud Van Giruet

Elemental Gelade I / Mayumi Azuma

Elemental Gelade Vol. 1

Created by Mayumi Azuma

Translation - Alethea Nibley
English Adaptation - Jordan Capell
Copy Editor - Peter Ahlstrom
Retouch and Lettering - Jose Macasocol, Jr.
Production Artist - Fawn Lau
Graphic Designer - James Lee

Editor - Troy Lewter
Digital Imaging Manager - Chris Buford
Production Manager - Liz Brizzi
Managing Editor - Lindsey Johnston
VP of Production - Ron Klamert
Editor-in-Chief - Rob Tokar
Publisher - Mike Kiley
President and C.O.O. - John Parker
C.E.O. and Chief Creative Officer - Stuart Levy

A TOKYOPOP® Manga

TOKYOPOP Inc.
5900 Wilshire Blvd. Suite 2000
Los Angeles, CA 90036

E-mail: info@TOKYOPOP.com
Come visit us online at www.TOKYOPOP.com

© 2002 MAYUMI AZUMA. All Rights Reserved.
First published in Japan in 2002 by MAG Garden Corporation.
English translation rights arranged with MAG Garden Corporation.
English text copyright © 2006 TOKYOPOP Inc.

All rights reserved. No portion of this book may be reproduced or transmitted in any form or by any means without written permission from the copyright holders. This manga is a work of fiction. Any resemblance to actual events or locales or persons, living or dead, is entirely coincidental.

ISBN: 1-59816-598-4

First TOKYOPOP printing: July 2006
10 9 8 7 6 5 4 3 2 1
Printed in the USA

Volume 1

by
Mayumi Azuma

TOKYOPOP®

HAMBURG // LONDON // LOS ANGELES // TOKYO

Contents

Re - No: 1 The Airship Red Lynx–Billowing Wind and Song–(Part One) 05

Re - No: 2 The Airship Red Lynx–Billowing Wind and Song–(Part Two) 58

Re - No: 3 The Great Windmill Elé Blanca–Artificial Calm 106

Re - No: 4 The Great Windmill Elé Blanca–The Introductory Beacon 142

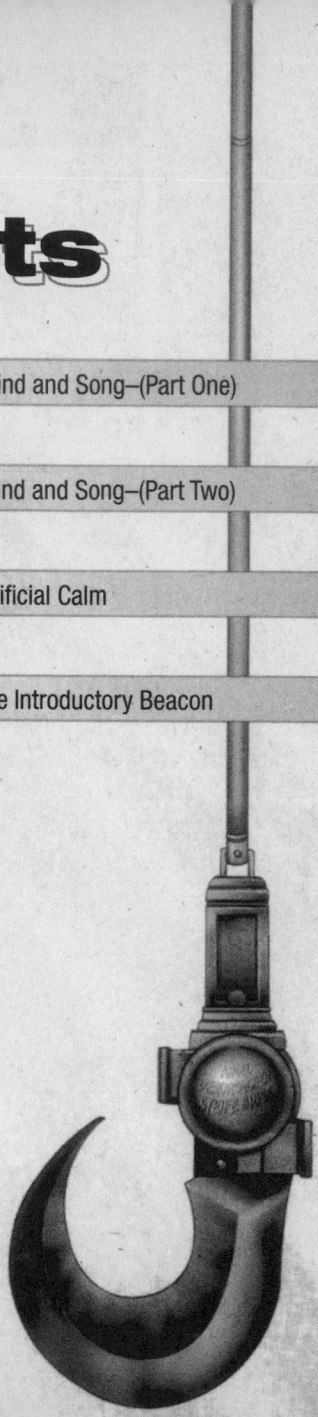

ギギ
LET'S SEE WHAT'S INSIDE...
THIS BOX IS COVERED IN DUST... LOOKS LIKE THE LOCK HAS RUSTED AWAY, TOO.
WHAT'S THIS?
JEWELS? GOLD COINS?
IT'S A GIRL?!
MY GOD...
?!!

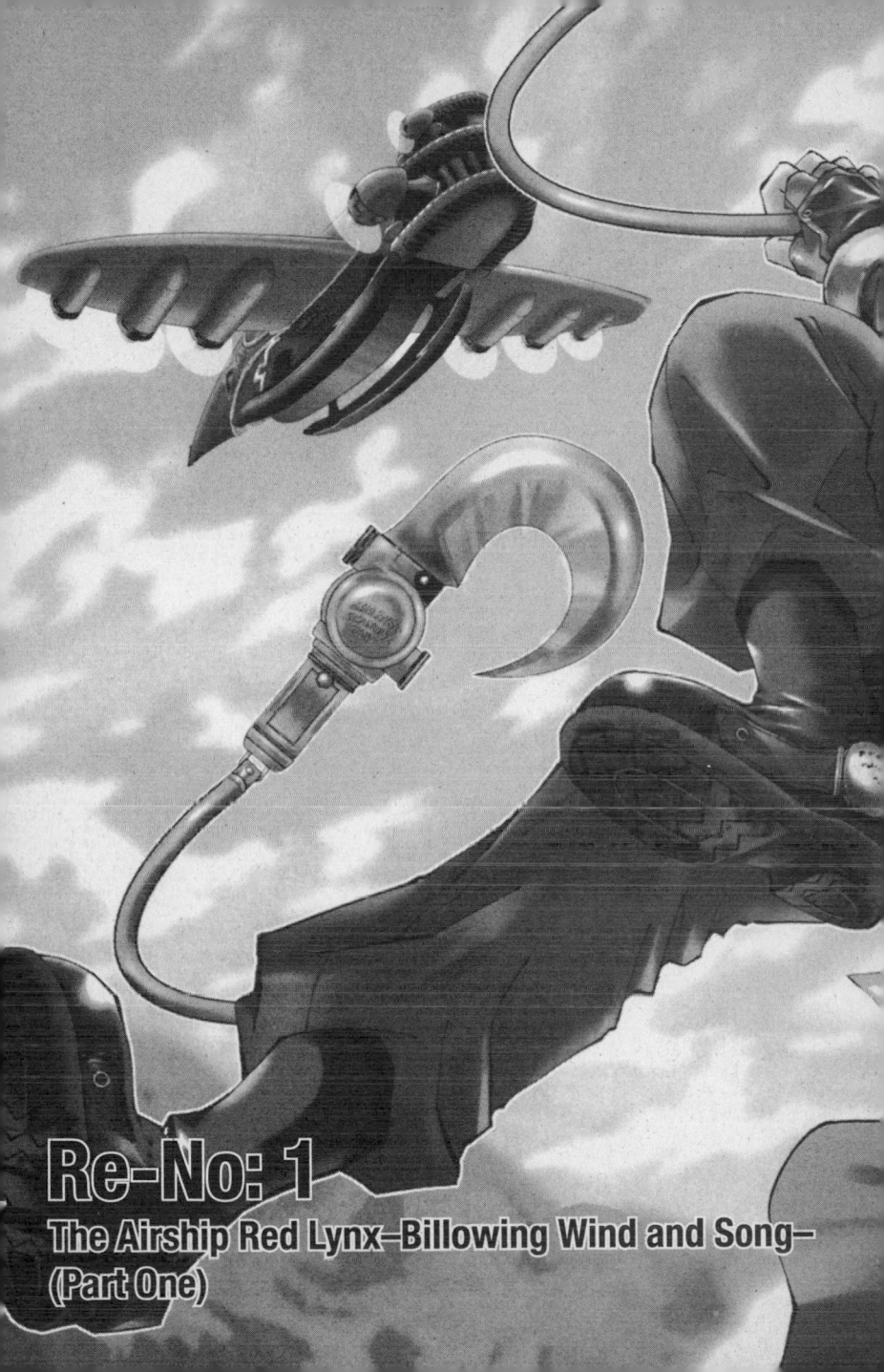

Re-No: 1

The Airship Red Lynx–Billowing Wind and Song– (Part One)

ゴオオオ

Hmph!
THEY'RE LATE...
I TOLD THEM TO BE HERE BY FIVE!
NOBODY HAS CALLED, SIR.
SIR, I THINK YOU SHOULD SEE THIS.
MY GOOD-NESS...!
THAT THING HAS ALWAYS CREEPED ME OUT.
BUT I STILL CAN'T BELIEVE THEY'RE WILLING TO PAY SO MUCH FOR THAT RATTY OLD DOLL.
WHAT? IS IT A GIANT BAT OR SOME-THING?

!!!!
KYAAAAAAAHH!!

ガッ
ンッ

パラ
パラ
HUNH...
BOW DOWN TO THE SKY PIRATE CREW, RED LYNX!
YOU HAVE GROWN FAT OFF YOUR OWN GREED ...
...SO WE'VE COME TO PUT YOU ON A DIET!
UH-HUH. I GET IT. NOW CAN YOU PLEASE GET OFF ME?
AH, SORRY...

WHAT ARE YOU DOING, COU?!
AH! HEY!
WAIT A SECOND!
DON'T LEAVE ME!!
WE'RE DONE HERE!
WE NEED TO GO ALREADY!
EH?
P-please... get off me...

SEE YA!
AND THANKS FOR THE LOOT!!

GOOD EVENING. WE'VE COME TO COLLECT THE ITEM WE DISCUSSED. ♡
WHAT ?!
MASTER! THE TREASURY IS EMPTY!
RED LYNX...
SO THAT WAS THE INFAMOUS SKY PIRATE CREW...
WHAT?
I'M SORRY, MADAME, BUT IT APPEARS YOU ARE ONE SECOND TOO LATE.
Empty?!
SOMEONE BEAT YOU TO IT.
THE DOLL...

SO, THEN I SEZ TO HIM...
...BUT YOU CAN'T SLIP PAST THE CLAWS OF THE RED LYNX CREW!"
..."YOU EVIL RATS MAY ESCAPE FROM THE EYES OF THE LAW WITH YOUR DIRTY TRICKS...

"PLEASE! SPARE MY LIFE!"
AND THEN THE MASTER OF THE HOUSE'S FACE GOT ALL TWISTED AND CRUMPLED LIKE THIS, AND HIS BODY STARTED TO SHAKE!
"YOU CAN HAVE ALL MY TREASURE, JUST DON'T HURT ME!"
BUT I, LIKE THE GENTLEMAN I AM...
OOF!!

WHAT?!
THAT'S A PRETTY BIG STORY FROM A GREENHORN WHO CAN'T EVEN PILOT A SHIP.
DON'T GET SO CARRIED AWAY.
I CAN TOO PILOT A SHIP...!
Owie...
SCFF
YEAH! MORE LIKE AGGRESSIVE STEERING!
YEAH, BUT YOU SUCK AT IT!
I HARDLY CALL IT PILOTING.

OH YEAH... AND I CRASHED THE ESCAPE POD.
I did this, and that...
I REMEMBER THE TIME I RAMMED THE LIGHTSHIP INTO THE CALMSHIP.
Part two.
I KNOW IT TOOK ME A LITTLE BIT TO GET USED TO IT, BUT I DID...!
Cou's flashback-- part one.
EVERYBODY'S MAKING FUN OF ME.
I CAN SO PILOT A SHIP!
WHAT?!
MAY AS WELL TAKE A PEEK WHILE I'M HERE...
I WONDER HOW WE DID TODAY?
NO WAY!
SOMEONE LEFT THE TREASURY DOOR OPEN!
SOMEBODY COULD TAKE ALL OUR LOOT.

SURE IS SOME WEIRD STUFF IN HERE...
Who'd want this crap?
WHOA...

WHAT'S THIS?
THIS BOX IS COVERED IN DUST... LOOKS LIKE THE LOCK HAS RUSTED AWAY, TOO.

ギ
ギ
ギ

GOLD COINS?
JEWELS?
LET'S SEE WHAT'S INSIDE...

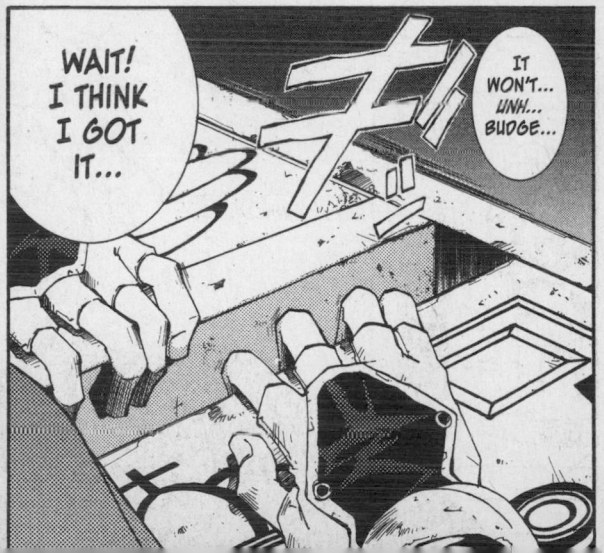
WAIT! I THINK I GOT IT...
IT WON'T... UNH... BUDGE...
ギ

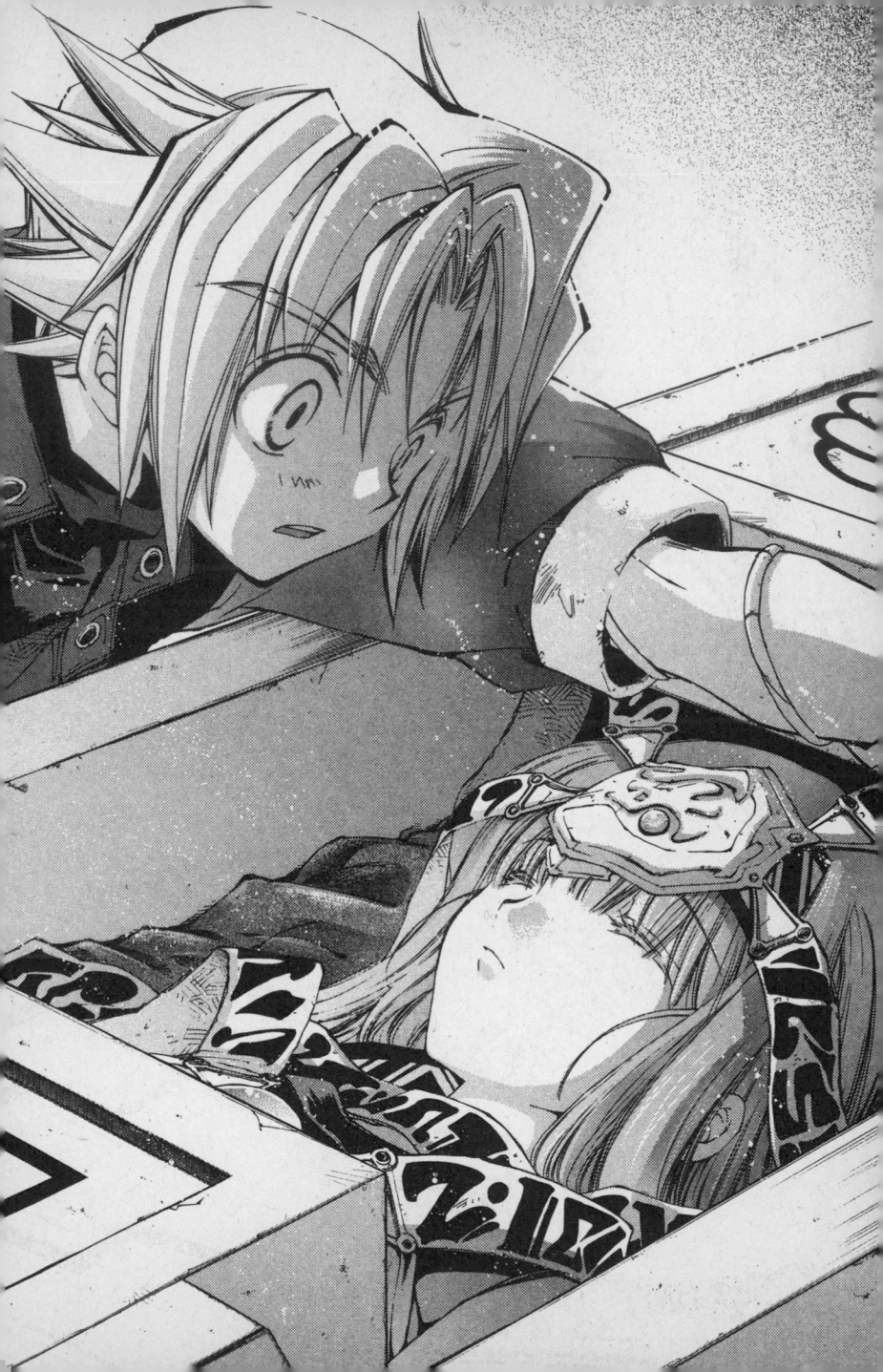

MY GOD...
IT'S A GIRL ?!

THEN AGAIN, SHE IS PRETTY INTRICATE.
FOR A SECOND THERE, I THOUGHT SHE WAS A REAL PERSON.
THAT CAN'T BE!
THERE'S NO WAY A PERSON WOULD BE INSIDE THIS FILTHY OLD BOX!
BUT I HAVEN'T BEEN ALONE WITH A GIRL IN TEN YEARS!
WHAT AM I DOING? IT'S JUST A DOLL...
EVEN SO... SHE IS CUTE...
はっ...
I GUESS THERE'S NO HARM IN GETTING A BETTER LOOK... HEH HEH...

HER BREASTS ARE SO... SO...
HER EYELASHES ARE SO LONG!!
HER SKIN IS SO WHITE...
BLINK

I DIDN'T MEAN IT!!
WAAAAAHH!
I'M SORRY!!
HUH...?
Y-YOU'RE... MOVING?!
ハ?!

TH-
THIS...
...THIS
CAN'T
BE...
YOU'RE
ALIVE?!

IF WE LET THEM GET AWAY, WE'LL NEVER HAVE ANOTHER CHANCE!!
WE KNOW WHERE SHE IS!!
NO!!
UM, DO YOU THINK YOU COULD SLOW DOWN A BIT...?
IN FACT, I THINK I'M GOING TO HAVE TO SPEED UP!
YEE-HAAA!!

しょぼ~
.....
THOSE ?
ARE YOU THE ONE WHO TOOK THESE OFF?
.....
ボー
EXCUSE ME, MISS...BUT WHY WERE YOU IN THAT BOX?
ブツ
ブツ
YES.
THANK YOU ANYWAY.
I GUESS I SHOULD HAVE ASKED FIRST.
I THOUGHT THEY WERE PART OF YOUR DECORA-TIONS.

EDEL GARDEN.
I GUESS I'LL BE GOING NOW.
コツ
コツ
WHAT?!
GOING?
GOING WHERE ?!

WHAT?
I AM GOING TO OPEN THE DOOR AND GO OUTSIDE.
HEY!!
WHAT DO YOU THINK YOU'RE DOING ?!
YOU CAN'T OPEN THAT!
BYE.
?!!
WHAT AM I SAYING ?!
MAKES PERFECT SENSE...
OF COURSE. THE FIRST STEP IS ALWAYS TO GO OUTSIDE...
Mm-hm.
DON'T OPEN THAT!!

NOT TO STATE THE OBVIOUS...
...BUT WE'RE NOT ON THE GROUND!
EH?

I'LL TAKE YOU THERE.
I'LL TAKE YOU TO EDEL GARDEN.
IT'S NOT SAFE FOR A GIRL BY HERSELF OUT HERE.
I MEAN, THERE'S NO TELLING WHAT COULD HAPPEN TO YOU ON THE WAY.

NO MATTER WHAT?
BUT... WHY?
NO.
OKAY, HERE'S A PLAN...
WHY? IS IT TOP SECRET OR SOMETHING?
I CAN'T TELL YOU.
She's getting me all excited!

WE TRAVEL ALL OVER THIS CONTINENT, AND I'VE NEVER HEARD OF IT.
MAYBE IT'S ON ANOTHER CONTINENT?
IF THAT'S THE CASE, I CAN'T EVEN GUESS HOW FAR AWAY IT IS...OR HOW MANY DAYS IT WOULD TAKE TO GET THERE.
HOWEVER FAR AWAY...
HOWEVER MANY DAYS IT TAKES, IT'S FINE.
THAT'S FINE.
NO MATTER WHAT, I HAVE TO GO THERE.
I HAVE TO GET TO EDEL GARDEN.

YOU MEAN... WE'RE IN A FLYING MACHINE?!
YEP. THERE'S TONS OF 'EM THESE DAYS.

Was it m-my imagination...or are we...flying?
N-no, it wasn't your imagination ...
We are INDEED flying...
Pant!
Huff!

MY GOODNESS...
A FLYING MACHINE?
WAIT...YOU'VE NEVER BEEN IN AN AIRSHIP BEFORE, HAVE YOU?
WHAT, HAVE YOU BEEN IN A BOX YOUR WHOLE LIFE?

WOULD YOU MIND DROPPING ME OFF, THEN?
WELL, SURE, BUT...
...I DON'T KNOW WHERE EDEL GARDEN IS.

I WILL BE FINE.
さらり
BESIDES, THIS HAS NOTHING TO DO WITH YOU.
I KNEW SHE'D SAY THAT...
ブオオオオ
EVERYBODY HAS STUFF THEY NEED TO DO... EVERYBODY HAS A CALLING...
EVEN YOU.
OKAY...
WITH THE PIRATES?!
I...I GUESS YOU'RE RIGHT.
BESIDES, I...
...DO NOT WANT HELP FROM...

I HAVE TO GO ASK THE BOSS.
LET'S GO.
しょぼ
Sleepy...
しょぼ
FROM WHAT?
?
EVERY-BODY HAS A CALLING...
AS FAR BACK AS I CAN REMEMBER, I NEVER HAD ANY PARENTS.
I HAD TO THIEVE AND STEAL JUST TO SURVIVE.

...BUT I'VE NEVER REALLY THOUGHT ABOUT IT BEFORE NOW.
I'VE SURE HAD MY SHARE OF FUN WITH MY FELLOW PIRATES...
WHEN I WAS FIVE, THE BOSS OF THE RED LYNX CREW TOOK ME IN.
WHAT'S MY CALLING?
WHOA!!
WHAT WAS THAT?!
HOLY COW!!

BOSS!! WHAT'S GOIN' ON?!
IDIOT! WHERE HAVE YOU BEEN?!
WE'RE BEING ATTACKED!
NO, THAT'S NOT IT!
I FELT A BUMP...! IS IT ENGINE TROUBLE ?!
ATTACKED?!

THEY'RE AMAZINGLY FAST AND AGILE!
DON'T TELL ME THE NATIONAL AIR GUARD HAS COME...!
DANG! I'VE NEVER SEEN A BATTLESHIP THAT SMALL BEFORE...!
DON'T BE STUPID! WOULD THAT BUNCH OF LILY-LIVERED MILITARY PANSIES COME AFTER US WITH JUST ONE SHIP?

ちょこん
I'LL GO AFTER THEM IN A LIGHT SHIP!
WITH YOUR LOUSY FLYING? PFFT! YOU'D ONLY GET IN THE WAY!
COVER THE OTHERS WITH THE SHIP'S CANNONS.
THERE'S NO TIME TO LOSE --!!
HURRY AND READY THE--
COU!
HOW DARE YOU BRING A WOMAN ON THE BRIDGE AT A TIME LIKE THIS!!
Muh weh ha hah!
NEVER MIND...! I'LL TELL YOU LATER!
WAIT...!
I CAN EXPLAIN!

ARE THEY INSANE?! THEY'RE GOING TO RAM US!!
THEY'RE COMING AROUND!
DAMN!!

WHEW!
SORRY TO HAVE TO BARGE IN LIKE THIS! ♡
WE ARE THE SOCIETY FOR THE COMPLETE PROTECTION OF EDEL RAIDS, ARC AILE.

EDEL...
...RAIDS?
PROTECTION SOCIETY?
YES!
I BELIEVE YOU ACQUIRED ONE OF OUR EDEL ARTIFACTS IN YOUR RECENT PILLAGING.
Yum!
That ship was so cramped...!
SURELY YOU'RE JOKING...!
WHAT THE...? NEVER HEARD OF IT.

SHE'S RIGHT THERE.
SHE'S THE ARTIFACT.
.....
WE WERE SUPPOSED TO PICK HER UP FROM THE MASTER OF THAT MANOR TODAY... BUT YOU WERE ONE STEP AHEAD OF US.
WE IN ARC AILE HAVE BEEN SEARCHING FOR HER WHEREABOUTS FOR A LONG TIME.
WHAT? THIS GIRL?

I THINK YOU'LL FIND OUR OFFER GENEROUS.
...WE'RE PREPARED TO COMPENSATE YOU FOR YOUR TROUBLE.
SO, SINCE SHE IS A PIECE OF YOUR BOOTY...

HOW DOES FIFTY MILLION SOUND?
THAT WILL COVER THE HANDLING COST, AND YOU CAN REPAIR YOUR SHIP. COME TO THINK OF IT, YOU COULD PROBABLY BUY A NEW SHIP WITH THIS MUCH!

カタカタ
カタ
50,000,000
$50,000,
WHIRR

HERE'S A CHECK.
Whoa...
Fifty million?!

NO DEAL!!
WHAT DO YOU THINK SHE IS?!
WHA?!
WE'RE NOT IN THE BUSINESS OF SELLING PEOPLE!!

Sigh...
REALLY ...?
WELL, THAT'S UNFORTUNATE...
SHUT UP! I'M TELLING YOU, WE WON'T GIVE HER TO YOU!
PLEASE... JUST CALM DOWN AND THINK ABOUT THIS...
I DON'T CARE HOW MUCH MONEY YOU GIVE US!
BY MEETING US HALFWAY, YOU COULD GET A LARGE SUM OF MONEY, WHICH WOULD BE THE SAME AS GETTING A NEW SHIP.
AND WE WOULD ACCOMPLISH OUR MISSION AND ALL GET HUGE PROMOTIONS.
あわ
あわあわ
あわわ...
Promotions?
WELL, JUST REMEMBER THAT WE OFFERED YOU A PEACEFUL SOLUTION.
I ASSURE YOU THAT WE WILL NOT LET HER GO!

GUNS.
WE WILL FULFILL OUR MISSION, NO MATTER WHAT.
OH, I KNEW IT WOULD COME TO THIS...
AND HOW WILL WE DO THAT, YOU ASK?
YEAH. HOW?
WHAT'S YOUR SECRET WEAPON?

NOW, THEN...
WAAAHH!!
カリ
カリカリカリ
ON TO AGGRESSIVE NEGOTIATIONS... ♡

ドォォォ
カッ
SHE'S MAKING A MESS OUT OF THINGS!
BOSS, IF SHE KEEPS THIS UP, WE'LL BE IN BIG TROUBLE!
BOSS !!!
...ABOUT THE EDEL RAIDS.
WAIT... I THINK I RE-MEMBER READING ONCE...
SERI-OUSLY ?
NOT WHO... WHAT.
THEY'RE HUMAN WEA-PONS.
WHO THE HECK ARE THEY?

Teyah!
WHY, YOU --!!
YOU DON'T REALLY WANT TO UNLEASH KUEA IN A PLACE LIKE THIS, DO YOU?!
WHAT ?!
I CAN HANDLE THESE PIRATES ON MY OWN!!
YOU TWO... GET HER!
I'VE BEEN CRAMPED UP IN THAT SHIP FOREVER! I NEED TO RELIEVE SOME STRESS!
Mwuah ha!
ROWEN, THIS IS AN ORDER !!
YES, MA'AM!
Heh heh!
I-I SEE... PLEASE, F-FEEL FREE...

THEY SAY AN EDEL RAID...
...WILL TRANS-FORM HER BODY...
...AND BECOME ONE WITH A HUMAN.

BECOME ONE WITH A HUMAN?!
WHAT HAPPENS WHEN THEY DO THAT?
ONCE THE TRANSFORMATION IS COMPLETE...
...THEY ARE AN INVINCIBLE WEAPON.

THIS IS THE FIRST TIME I'VE SEEN IT WITH MY OWN EYES!
AMAZING!
A HUMAN MORPHING INTO A WEAPON?
NOW...
...HAND HER OVER TO US.

Re-No: 2

The Airship Red Lynx–Billowing Wind and Song– (Part Two)

I DON'T THINK SO!
?!!!
GYAAAAH!!
UNH!!

HURK...
JUST HAND HER OVER TO US AND NOBODY GETS HURT.
I REALLY DON'T WANT TO HAVE TO DO THIS.
STOP MAKING ME REPEAT MYSELF !!
SHUT UP!!
I SAID NO!!

NOTHING WE SAY TO THOSE KIDS IS GOING TO HELP.
ONCE WE ROUGH THEM UP A LITTLE, THEY'LL CHANGE THEIR TUNE.
I'M REALLY GETTING TIRED OF THIS.
KUEA?
LET'S GET IT OVER WITH!!
GRAAAAH!!
KUEA, DON'T!!

BOSS!!
COU!
HURRY!!
TAKE HER TO THE LIFEBOATS!

What do we do?
THEY'RE GETTING AWAY!
FOLLOW THEM!!
OKAY!
HOLD IT JUST ONE SECOND...
!!!
LET'S GO!!
I DON'T THINK WE'RE GONNA LET YOU GO.
NOT UNTIL YOU APOLOGIZE FOR WHAT YOU'VE DONE TO OUR SHIP.

DON'T WORRY... THIS DOOR IS VERY STRONG.
NOT EVEN A BOMB COULD BLOW IT OPEN.
A bomb?

カリ
ッ

OUR CALMSHIP'S LOSING STABILITY!
BUT IT'S OKAY. IF YOU GO NOW, YOU CAN STILL GET OUT.
ギッ
ギッ

GET IN HERE.
I'M GOING TO SAVE YOU.

I JUST REMEMBERED...
...THIS A FLYING VEHICLE, RIGHT?
WHAT HAPPENS WHEN IT CAN'T FLY?

WHAT?
!
And hang on--it's gonna be a bit rough...
HURRY!
THAT'S NOT YOUR CONCERN.
LET'S GET MOVING!
I DESPISE HUMANS.
NO.
BUT...
...GETTING ALL OF YOU INVOLVED AND THEN RUNNING AWAY?
I COULDN'T LIVE WITH THAT.

I AM SURE THE REASON THOSE PEOPLE ARE TRYING TO CATCH ME...
...IS THE SAME REASON THAT PEOPLE SEALED ME UP.
IT'S ALL RIGHT.
YOU CAN GIVE ME TO THOSE PEOPLE.
HUH?!
REASON?
WHAT POSSIBLE REASON WOULD JUSTIFY THAT?!
MY POWER IS TOO STRONG.

THE GREATER THE POWER...
WHAT IS THAT?
...THE STRONGER AND MORE DANGEROUS THE WEAPON.
LOOK AT HER HEAD...!
A GREEN...
I CAN'T BE ALLOWED TO JUST WANDER AROUND WITH THIS MUCH POWER.
I'D END UP HURTING SOMEONE.
...STONE?!
I AM AN EDELRAID.
FOR HUMANS, OUR POWER BECOMES A WEAPON.

YOU GOTTA BE KIDDING ME!
YOU CAN TEAR DOWN THAT HUGE STEEL DOOR?!
IT'S FRIGHTENING, ISN'T IT?
TO THINK...
...I CAN DO ALL THAT.

WHAT?!
SO? THAT DOESN'T MATTER.
NO BUTS. EVERYBODY HAS A CALLING.
YOU SAID THAT TO ME.
NOW GET IN.
IT DOESN'T MATTER.
HUH ...?
BUT ...!

WHEN I WAS A KID, I DID BAD STUFF ALL THE TIME.
ALL I DID WAS GET INTO FIGHTS AND STEAL THINGS.
I WAS FIVE WHEN THE SKY PIRATES TOOK ME IN. BUT NOW, TEN YEARS LATER, THE BOSS STILL TELLS ME I'M JUST A GREENHORN.
AND SO...
...I THOUGHT ABOUT IT.
I THOUGHT ABOUT WHAT SOMEONE LIKE ME MIGHT NEED TO DO EARN MY STRIPES.
HEH...
BUT I COULDN'T THINK OF ANYTHING.

...YOU HAVE SOME-THING.
BUT...
BUT YOU REFUSED.
Oof!
SO I OFFERED TO BE YOUR BODY-GUARD.
YOU'RE GOING, AREN'T YOU?
TO EDEL GARDEN?

NO, YOU CAN'T!
WELL, I'M A MEMBER OF RED LYNX, TOO.
Ah! OH, YEAH ...!
SO I'LL HOLD THEM HERE AS LONG AS I CAN.
TELL ME YOUR NAME.
ONE LAST THING ...
I DON'T WANT TO CALL YOU "EDEL" ANYTHING ...

BUT YOU CAN CALL ME REN.
I HATE LONG NAMES.
ME, TOO.
... REVERIE.
REVERIE METHER-LENCE.
IT'S...
REN...
BE CARE-FUL OUT THERE.
PEOPLE CALL ME COU.
BUT MY FULL NAME IS COUD VAN GIRUET.
COU.

I DON'T KNOW HOW TO MOVE THIS THING.
I CAN'T.
COU!!
ESPECIALLY WITH JUST THAT HOOK.
BESIDES, YOU'D BE NO MATCH FOR AN EDEL RAID.
!
COU?
WILL YOU COME WITH ME?
PLUS...
REN...
...YOU SAID...
...THAT YOU WOULD TAKE ME TO EDEL GARDEN.

IF YOU DO...
...I'LL LEND YOU MY POWER.
SURE.
I'LL GO WITH YOU.

ROWEN!!
YOU HEARD HER, KUEA!
HURRY! THEY'RE GETTING AWAY!
THERE'S NO DOOR I CAN'T BREACH!
ALMOST THERE!
OH NO! THE DOOR!
WAH!
twist
REN?

WHAT THE --?!
WHAT ARE YOU DOING?!

Slowly concealed, revealed...
Spinning together into the ephemeral night...
Thoughts expressed, shining in jewel-like eyes.
...let us be brought together and exchange...
...as long as we both shall live.
Clad in turbulent wind...

Our vow of souls intertwined.

ONE HIT SHOULD DO THE TRICK!
AAAHH!!

REVERIE METHERLENCE HAS TAKEN WEAPON FORM. THE LAST IN THE METHERLENCE LINE...
...ONE OF THE SEVEN GLITTERING JEWELS!

I WON'T!
NO, NO, NO WAY IN HELL!
SHE'LL TEAR ME APART...!
キリリリ
WIMPS!
GACK!
Just a... wait...
GET HER, ROWEN!
MY BLADE IS AS SHARP AND AS SWIFT AS THE WIND.
IT CAN CUT THROUGH STEEL LIKE PAPER.
COU...
OH, WOW...
AND IT'S AS LIGHT AS A FEATHER...
THIS IS MY POWER AS AN EDEL RAID.

I'LL DO IT MYSELF!
FINE!
I AM NOT AFRAID!

MIS-SILES?
.....?
SOME STRANGE THINGS ARE COMING TOWARD US.
THEY'RE MISSILES!
JUST CUT THROUGH THEM.
IDIOT! YOU CAN'T JUST CUT THROUGH THEM!

AAAHH!
WOW!
WHAT WAS THAT?!
IT SCARED ME SO MUCH I LET GO OF YOU.
I TOLD YOU NOT TO CUT THEM!
OH NO!! THE SHIP!!

BOSS! WE'RE LOSING ALTITUDE, FAST!
WAAAH!!
BOSS?!
YOU GO THROUGH OUR LOOT WITHOUT PERMISSION, YOU DESTROY OUR SHIP...
I CAN'T AFFORD THE EXTRA WEIGHT IN MY CREW!
SHUT UP!!
WAIT! WHAT ABOUT YOU?

AT LEAST YOU'VE GOT YOUR PRIORITIES STRAIGHT.
BUT YOU TOOK THE WOMAN OVER THE MONEY.
B--
BOSS...
PROTECT HER.
BE A MAN, COU.

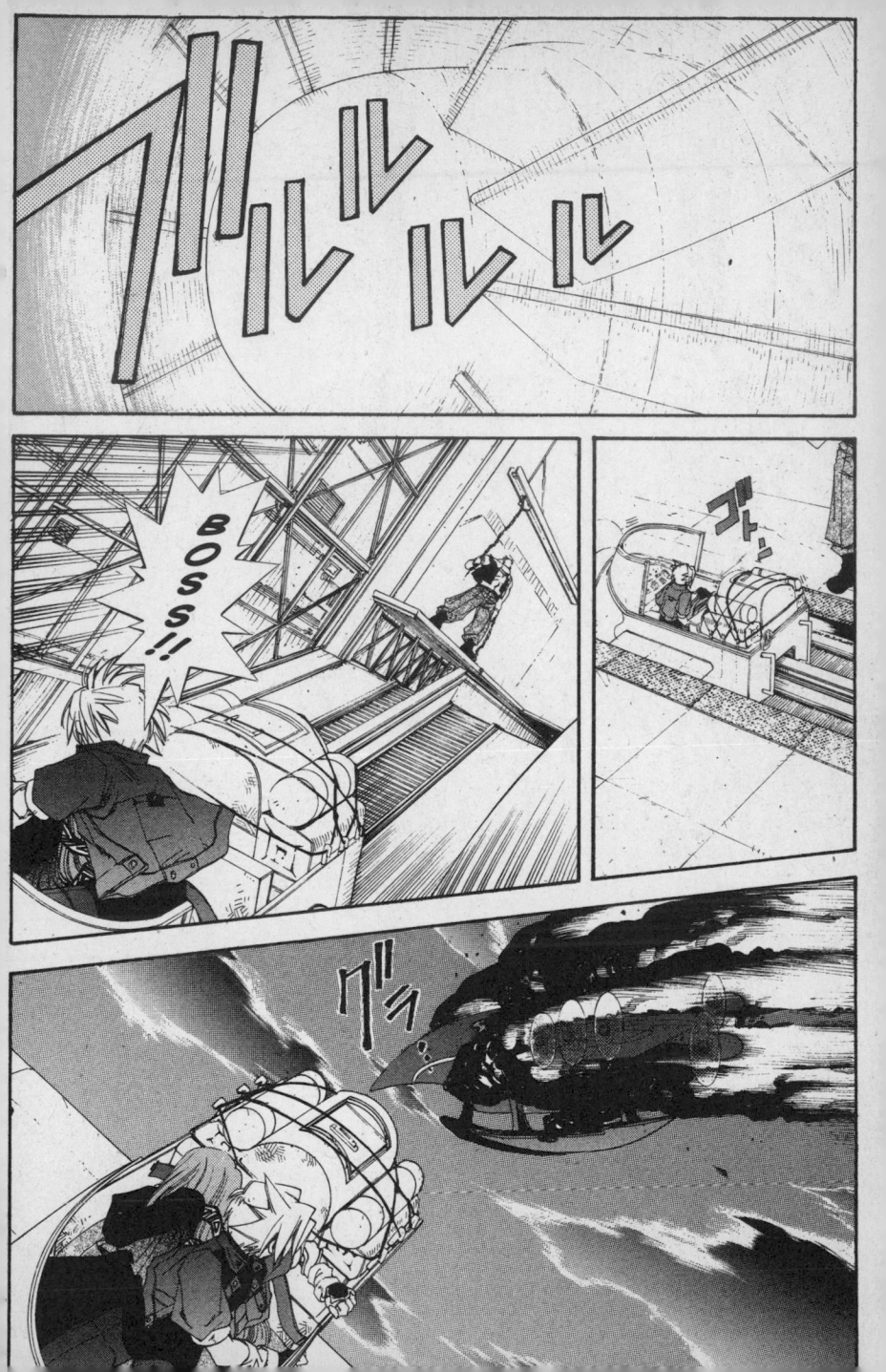
ルルルルル
BOSS!!
ゴト
グラ

NOOOOO!!

WHY?
WHY?!
NO ...
EVERY-ONE...
WHAT, REN?
OVER THERE!

HA HA!
THOSE GUYS...
NICE JOKE!
HM?
BEHIND ...?
LOOK BEHIND ME?
OKAY.
We're flying...

AAGGH!!
NOOO!!
WE HAVE TO GET HER WHILE THEY'RE SEPARATED!
WHAT ARE YOU GOING TO DO?
It's so frustrating!
.....
Leave it to me!
CAN YOU MAKE THIS THING MOVE, COU?
THESE GUYS SURE ARE PERSIS-TENT.
Here they come again!

DAH!!
ダダダダダダ
I'LL FIRE A WARNING SHOT TO GET THEM TO STOP.
ペロペロ
?!!
FIRE!
Scary!
YOU SAID YOU WERE GOING TO FIRE A WARNING SHOT.
I DID! THEY FLEW RIGHT INTO IT!
ドゴォォォ

BUT THEY'RE FALLING HEAD-FIRST...!
COW!!
THEY BOTH MADE IT!
BOSS!
IDIOT KID COULDN'T PILOT A SHOPPING CART!
DANGIT... THEY'VE REALLY DONE IT NOW!

OW!
WAAAAAH!!
THIS JUST CAME FLYING IN.
CAN'T YOU SEE I'M A LITTLE BUSY RIGHT NOW?
UM, BOSS ...?
WHAT IS IT?
!!!
NOW THAT WAS A CLOSE ONE...
EXCUSE ME! WOULD YOU PLEASE NOT HANG FROM OUR SHIP WITHOUT ASKING?
AAAAAAAAAAAAAAAAAA
Our... propeller?

ARE YOU OKAY, REN?
HEY!
ズズズ。
ピキピキ
SHE'S ASLEEP...
ちら
REN!

DON'T YOU WANT TO WAKE UP FOR THAT?
WE'RE GOING TO EDEL GARDEN NOW, AREN'T WE?
HUP...
WHAT DO YOU WANT?
AND I'M NOT GIVING YOU REN.
SHE'S USED UP TOO MUCH POWER. I THINK SHE'S RECHARGING.

OKAY. LATER, GUYS.
すたすた
…
PLEASE, DON'T BE SO DEFENSIVE…!
AS YOU CAN SEE, OUR SHIP IS BROKEN, TOO.
WE CAN'T TAKE HER WITH US LIKE THIS.
FATE HAS THRUST US TOGETHER.
A LOT HAS HAPPENED, BUT WHAT'S IMPORTANT IS THAT WE'RE ALL SAFE.
…WAIT!
WAIT…
…WAIT…
KUEA. NICE TO MEET YOU. ♡
I'M ROWEN.
I'M CISQUA. PLEASED TO MEET YOU!
WE, ARC AILE, WILL ACCOMPANY YOU.

OUR AIRSHIP IS BROKEN AND WE CAN'T GET BACK TO HEAD-QUARTERS.
IF WE CAN'T COLLECT HER, WE HAVE NO CHOICE BUT TO MONITOR HER.
UM, BOSS?
OF COURSE I'M SERIOUS.
ARE YOU SERIOUS?
BESIDES, I HEARD SOMETHING.
I KNOW THE PLACE THEY'RE HEADING.
EDEL GARDEN, THE LAND OF WEALTH AND PROSPERITY.
AND I'VE HEARD OF POLITICAL UNREST THERE.

WOW! YOU REALLY KNOW HOW TO MAKE LEMONADE OUT OF LEMONS, BOSS!
IT MIGHT FINALLY GET US OUR PROMOTIONS.
PERHAPS WE CAN USE THIS INFORMATION.
Huh huh huh...
Huh huh ...
WHAT DO YOU MEAN, WE DON'T HAVE ANY MONEY?!
I can't breathe!
DIDN'T WE RECEIVE A LOT OF MONEY FROM HEADQUARTERS WHEN WE LEFT?!
SO WE COULDN'T GO BACK ANYWAY.
NEVER GIVE UP!
BESIDES, WE LOST ALL OUR MONEY.
HUH?!

WELL, IT ALL BURNED UP.
ゴオオオオ

HEY, CISQUA.
Koff koff!
ゲホゲホ
SORRY TO INTERRUPT...

...BUT IT LOOKS LIKE THE KIDS ARE GONE.
AAAH!!

WHAT?!
PLEASE WAIT!
I TOLD YOU NOT TO FOLLOW US!
す

IT'S A PRETTY GOOD PRICE FOR NORMAL GIRLS.
OH, REALLY?
THIS IS CHICKEN FEED.
ドサ
IF YOU WANT MORE MONEY, JUST CAPTURE ONE OF THOSE.
YEAH, RIGHT.
AN EDEL RAID.
IT'S NOT LIKE YOU JUST COME ACROSS ONE OF THOSE EVERY DAY.

Re-No: 3

The Great Windmill Elé Blanca–Artificial Calm

ドンッ
GROWL
NO NO NO
GROWL

ROAR!!
I'M HUNGRY!!
BOSS, IF WE DON'T GIVE KUEA SOMETHING TO EAT...
...SHE CAN'T RESTORE HER ABILITY TO CHANGE INTO A WEAPON.
FEED ME!!
growl
GROWL
DANG... THESE GUYS ARE ANNOYING.
GYAAAAHH!
SHE'S GOING TO EAT ME!
WAAAAAHH!!
ALL OF OUR RATIONS WERE DESTROYED.
WHO KNOWS WHAT WE COULD FIND IN THIS FOREST?

I CAN'T BELIEVE REN HASN'T EVEN TWITCHED WITH ALL THIS NOISE GOING ON.
SHE MUST BE REALLY TIRED.
RIGHT, COU, OLD BUDDY?!
Old buddy?
DON'T YOU AGREE?!
LISTEN!!
WE CAN'T BUY FOOD!
We can't check into a hotel!
NOT HAVING MONEY IS A MATTER OF LIFE OR DEATH!!

Eeeee!
I'M HUNGRY!!
きゅるるる
WHY DON'T WE JUST ROB SOMEBODY?
CAMP OUT OR SOMETHING.
I DON'T CARE. YOU WERE THE ONES THAT WANTED TO FOLLOW ME.
COU!
Ow ow ow!
DO YOU HEAR YOURSELF?!
ROB SOMEONE?!
NEVER!!
WE'RE SUPPOSED TO BE BETTER THAN THAT!
WE ARE A PROTECTION AGENCY! WE DON'T ROB PEOPLE!
OKAY!
FINE!

ガガ
ガ
ポロ
NO MATTER HOW BROKE I AM...
...I'LL BE RICH IN MY HEART.
I WILL NOT LOSE MY SENSE OF MORALITY!
Aahh...
BOSS, THAT'S BEAUTIFUL.
WAAAAAHH!!
HEY! LOOK OUT!
ドドド

EEK!
YOUR MONEY OR YOUR LIFE, PUNK!!

BOSS!!
QUIET, YOU!
YOU DO VALUE YOUR DAUGHTER'S LIFE, DON'T YOU?
FATHER ...?
FREEZE!
WHO THE HECK ARE YOU?
GULP!
NOW'S NOT THE TIME, GUYS!
LOOK OUT!!
SOME-THING'S COMING!!

ドガッ
ドガッ
ドガッ

IT LOOKS LIKE SOME SORT OF BEAR.
I THOUGHT THEY LIVED FURTHER NORTH.
FINALLY! YOU'RE AWAKE!
WHAT IS IT, REN?
GRAAAAH!!!

Crimson heart...
Don the wind...
...and make our vow!

WOW.
BEAR STEW...
GRAAW!
MAN... THAT WAS CLOSE.
THANKS, REN.

LET'S GO!!
COU, WAIT!
IF YOU RUN OFF BY YOUR-SELF...
ズズー
...I CAN'T LOCK ON TO THE TARGET!
WHAT?!
Unharmed
GRRAAAH!!

SIGH...
ドス
ドス
I DON'T NEED YOU!
ARE YOU ALL RIGHT?
I'M NOT THANKING YOU.
I COULD HAVE HANDLED THAT ON MY OWN.
WHAT DO YOU MEAN, YOU DON'T NEED US?!
THERE'S NO WAY YOU COULD HAVE KNOWN WHAT WAS GOING TO HAPPEN IF ROWEN HADN'T HELPED YOU!
NOT THAT I CARE IF YOU GET YOURSELF HURT...!
BOSS... MELLOW OUT.

JEEZ ...!
BUT WE NEED HER! IT'S OUR JOB TO MAKE SURE NOTHING HAPPENS TO HER!
REN !!
IT'S TOO EARLY TO KNOW EVERY-THING.
I'M SORRY YOU DIDN'T KNOW.
IT WAS JUST OUR SECOND TIME.

HEY, IS THERE A HOTEL NEARBY?
HUH?
SHE NEEDS SOME REST!
THANK YOU KINDLY.
WE'RE INDEBTED TO YOU.

I CAN'T LET HER SLEEP ON THE GROUND!
REN IS A GIRL!
YOU TOLD US TO "CAMP OUT"!
Yuck! Ptooi!

IT MAY NOT BE MUCH, BUT IT'S A PLACE TO REST.
SINCE YOU SAVED ME, FEEL FREE TO STAY AT MY HOUSE.
DAMMIT! I'M A GIRL, TOO!
Easy
GRR!

FATHER?
THANK YOU, SIR!
SERI-OUSLY?

I WISH WE HAD A MAP.
WHERE THE HECK ARE WE?
THIS IS KIND OF A LONELY PLACE.

WELL, WHAT DO YOU KNOW...! THERE WAS A TOWN RIGHT HERE!

IT'S A SMALL TOWN.
THIS IS ELĒ BLANCA.

SIR?
EXCUSE ME, SIR? WHAT DO YOU CALL THIS PLACE?

MY HOUSE IS AT THE BOTTOM OF THIS HILL.
HUH...?
WH-WHAT...
WHAT IS THAT?!

BUT... I DON'T FEEL ANY WIND.
...
THAT? WHY, THAT'S OUR TOWN'S WINDMILL.
YEAH ...
YOU'RE RIGHT.
NO WIND... HUH.
IS THAT WHY IT'S NOT MOVING?

しょぼしょぼ
DOES YOUR TOWN STILL USE THE WIND-MILL?
HM?
OH, NO.

WHEN I WAS A LITTLE GIRL...
...WE WOULD GRIND FLOUR AND DRAW WATER UTILIZING THE POWER OF THE WINDMILL.
Steam... power?
DOES IT WORK?
BUT CAN YOU SEE THE BUILDING STANDING ON THE OTHER SIDE OF THE WINDMILL?
IT'S A FORTRESS EQUIPPED WITH MACHINES THAT PRODUCE STEAM.
VERY WELL.
THOUGH THE PRICE FOR THE POWER IS HIGH...
...WE STILL NEED IT TO WORK.
STEAM POWER IS WHAT SUPPORTS THE JOBS OF THE TOWNS-PEOPLE.

THERE'S NOTHING WE CAN DO.
WE JUST HAVE TO ENDURE.
AS LONG AS THAT FORTRESS IS BLOCKING THE WIND, THE WINDMILL CAN'T TURN.
THE OWNER OF THE FORTRESS HOLDS THE REAL POWER IN THIS TOWN.
WE NEED HIM TO LIVE.
I'M AFRAID WE'RE ALL STUCK ...
...JUST LIKE THAT WINDMILL.

THIS WINDMILL WILL NEVER MOVE AGAIN.
I SEE...
WHY?

NOTHING CAN CATCH THE WIND...
...BY JUST SITTING AND WAITING.

GROWLL
SCRAPS?! YOU ATE MINE, TOO!
PLEASE...JUST TRY TO MAKE IT THROUGH THE NIGHT! WE'LL FIND SOMETHING ELSE TOMORROW, OKAY?!
With you making so much noise, I can't sleep either!
I'M STILL HUNGRY!
THOSE WERE JUST SCRAPS! I STILL FEEL LIKE I HAVEN'T EVEN EATEN!
TALK ABOUT ANNOYING...
THEY'RE STILL AT IT.
CHIONP
Gyaaaahh!!
REN?
UM... HEY...
.....
WELL, I'LL BE IN THE ROOM NEXT DOOR.
OKAY.

COU?
WILL YOU BE OKAY HERE ...
...ALL BY YOUR-SELF?
さらり
I'LL BE FINE.
O-OH! I SEE!
Ha ha!
YEAH.
GOOD NIGHT.
GOOD NIGHT.
キィ

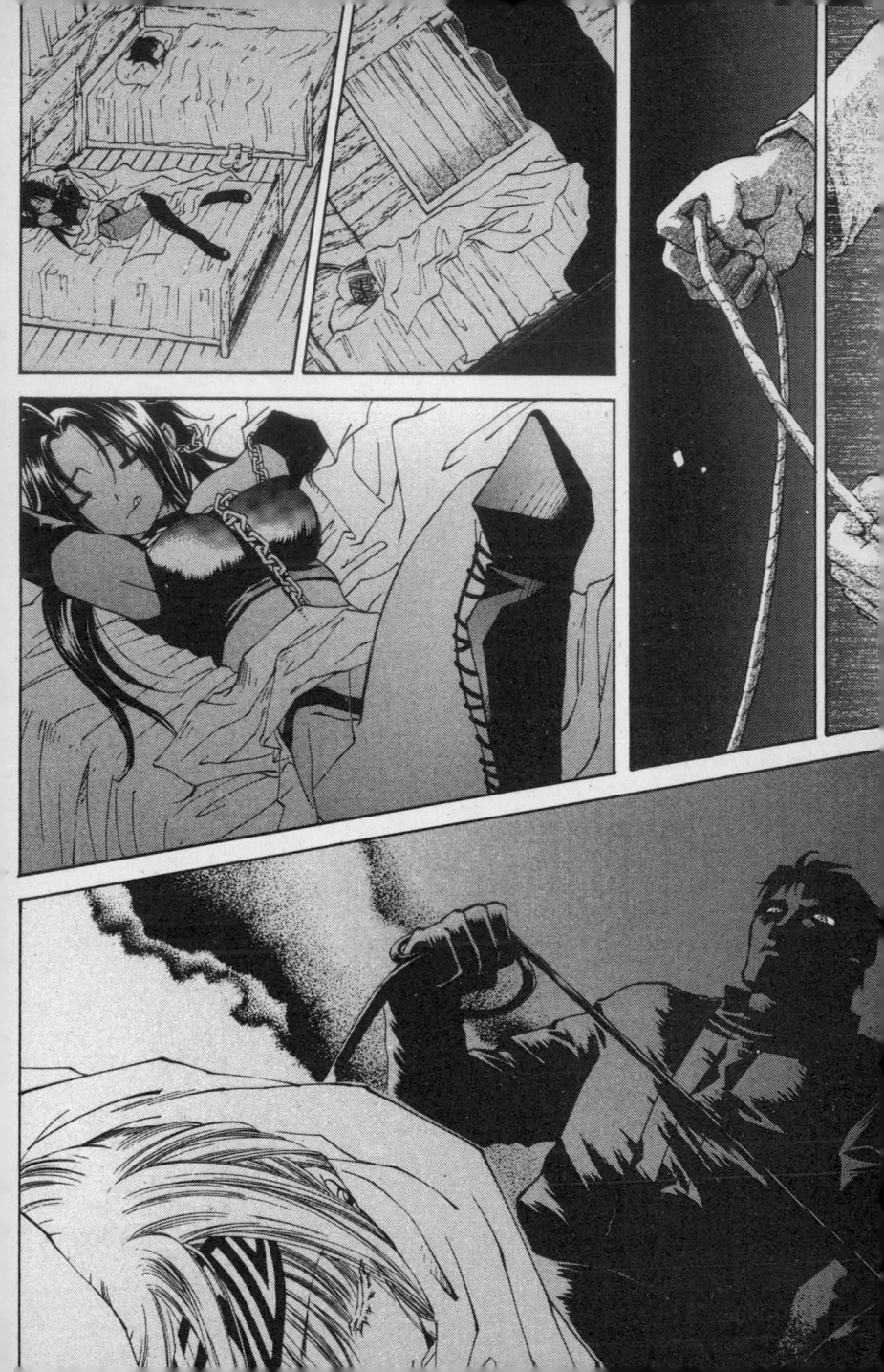

BOSS !!
WHAT'S GOING ON?!
WHAT WAS THAT NOISE ?!
STOP! PLEASE!!
OW OW OW OW!

HEY --!!
YOU!!

WHAT'S GOING ON?
GASP!
WHERE'S REN?
COU?
WHAT THE--?!
REN!!!

REN...

BEAZON?
IS SHE ONE?
LOOK AT HOW HARD SHE SLEEPS.
YES...
POOR LITTLE THING.

Re-No: 4

The Great Windmill Elé Blanca– The Introductory Beacon

WHAT'S GOING ON, MISTER?!
START TALKING!!
KUEA... WANT TO EAT HIM?
SURE. ♫
YIPE!

PLEASE, WAIT!!
DON'T BLAME MY FATHER!
FIORA, NO!
HE HAD NO CHOICE! HE DID IT TO SAVE ME...!
SAVE YOU?
OH, SURE... HAPPENS ALL THE TIME.
SO HE BUILT A TALL FORTRESS IN FRONT OF THE WINDMILL TO BLOCK THE WIND...
...AND MAKES YOU BUY STEAM POWER INSTEAD, TAKING YOUR DAUGHTERS IF YOU CAN'T PAY...
RIIIGHT ...

I MADE UP MY MIND THAT WE WOULD LEAVE TOWN... AND WE DID IT. WE EVEN MANAGED TO ESCAPE...
...BUT HIS GOONS FOUND US.
WE DON'T HAVE ANY MORE MONEY.
ALL I HAVE LEFT IS MY DAUGHTER FIORA.
IF SHE WERE TAKEN FROM ME...
I DIDN'T PLAN ON USING HER...
...BUT SHE WAS AN EDEL RAID.
SO YOU JUST GAVE THEM REN?!
HE'D TAKE HER...
I JUST COULDN'T LOSE MY DAUGHTER.

I'M SORRY !!
H-HE HAD NO CHOICE ...!
THERE WAS NOTHING WE COULD DO!
WAIT! COU!
DANG IT!!
YOU'RE NOT PLANNING TO GO OUT THERE BY YOURSELF, ARE YOU?!

ズズ
ミシッ
ガキ

HEH!
SMIRK
SUCCESS!
MAN... I AM GOOD ...!
I'M COMING FOR YOU, REN.

HUH?
THIS ISN'T WHERE I WENT TO SLEEP.
JUST HANG IN THERE...
MM-MM.
HI.
I SEE YOU'RE AWAKE.

AMAZING... YOU LOOK JUST LIKE A NORMAL LITTLE GIRL.

.....?!
SHOW ME!!
WHERE'S YOUR ELEMENTAL GELADE?!

WHERE IS IT?! WHERE'S THE PROOF THAT YOU'RE AN EDEL RAID?!
YOUR ELEMENTAL GELADE...
HEH HEH...
I THINK I FOUND IT...
I...I DON'T SEE IT...

DON'T TOUCH ME!!
NOOOO!!
NOOOO!!

AND A PRETTY ONE, TOO.
WE CAN GET A GOOD PRICE FOR YOU...
YOU ARE AN EDEL RAID.
Heh heh...

SORRY TO INTERRUPT YOUR FUN...
...BUT WE'VE GOT A MOUSE.

WHAT?!

BEAZON.

DANG IT... I HAVE TO HURRY AND SAVE REN.
I HOPE SHE'S ALL RIGHT.
YEP... I'M LOST.
IS IT SOMEHOW DIFFERENT IF SHE'S AN EDEL RAID?
IT'S TO SELL THEM.
ドキ
ドキ
WHAT?
Yay!
WHY DOES HE WANT TO TAKE GIRLS ANYWAY?
DOES HE JUST LIKE WOMEN THAT MUCH? DOES HE MAKE THEM SERVE HIM?
THAT OLD GUY WAS SAYING HE WANTS THEM MORE IF THEY'RE EDEL RAIDS.

EDEL RAIDS ARE RARE. THEY HAVE... UNIQUE ABILITIES.
There is, there is...!
There better be food here!
I HEARD THEM SAYING IT IN TOWN.
THE OWNER OF THIS FORTRESS DEALS IN THE BLACK MARKET.
THEY SAY HE'S MAKING A KILLING BY SELLING THE TOWN'S GIRLS AND CAPTURED EDEL RAIDS.
THEY'RE TRADED ON THE BLACK MARKET FOR LARGE AMOUNTS OF MONEY.
WAIT A MINUTE... DID YOU SAY MONEY?
DOES THAT MEAN REN'S ALREADY BEEN SOLD?!
WE KNOW THAT REN IS STILL INSIDE THIS BUILDING.
NOW, CALM DOWN.
YOU'RE RIGHT. THERE'S NO WAY THAT YOU, COU, HAVING BEEN TRAINED BY SKY PIRATES...
...WOULD HAVE GOTTEN LOST, IS THERE?
WHAT ARE YOU DOING HERE ANYWAY?! I DON'T NEED YOUR HELP!
Heh.
TH-THAT'S RIGHT! O-OF COURSE NOT!
Burn.

IT DETECTS ANY EDEL RAID WITHIN A ONE KM RADIUS.
CHECK IT OUT...I'VE ALREADY INPUTTED REN'S DATA.

TADAH!!
ARC AILE
THE EDEL RAID RADAR THAT ARC AILE PROVIDES TO THE GOVERNMENT!

SO WHAT'S THIS FUZZY GUY?

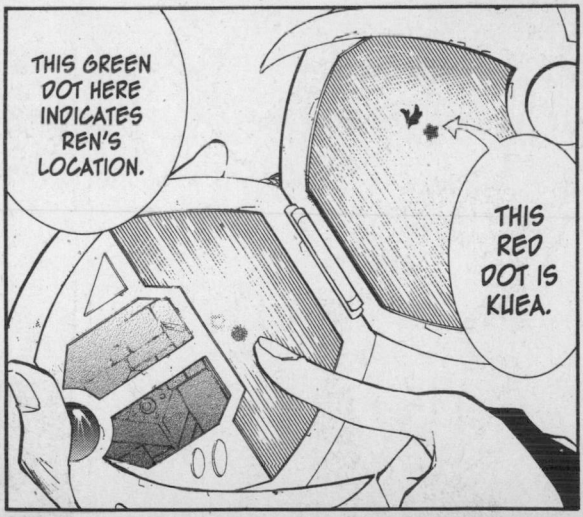
THIS GREEN DOT HERE INDICATES REN'S LOCATION.
THIS RED DOT IS KUEA.

THAT MEANS THAT INSIDE THIS BUILDING ...
REN WAS THE ONLY ONE THE TOWNSPEOPLE GAVE HIM.
BUT HE WOULDN'T KEEP HIS MERCHANDISE JUST LYING AROUND....
FOLKS, THE ENEMY...

EH?

WHAT, THIS COLOR-LESS LIGHT ...?
IT'S AN UNIDENTIFIED EDEL RAID!
By the way, the first edition came with a carrying case.

WE HAVE KUEA!!
BUT NEVER FEAR !!
ば
ば
THAT'LL SHOW HIM!!

...IS AN EDEL RAID PLEASURE.

WHERE DID SHE GO?!
ごうぜん。
WHAT?! SHE'S GONE?!

BUT BOSS, IF HE CAN USE AN EDEL RAID...
Grrr...
...WE MIGHT END UP HAVING TO FIGHT ONE.

KUEA, AT A TIME LIKE THIS, HOW CAN YOU--
ENJOY ALL THIS DELISH FOOD? EASY... LIKE THIS! ♬

WE SHOULD LET KUEA FILL UP SO SHE'S READY TO FIGHT.
AW...I GUESS YOU'RE RIGHT.

チカッ
チカ
ヒタ…
WHOA...DID YOU S-SEE THAT?
YEAH.
?!!
THIS WAS YOUR DINNER, WAS IT?
ぽりぽり
OH... I GET IT. ♪

ARE YOU SERIOUS ?!
DUDE, IT'S GOT TO BE ILLEGAL TO KEEP PETS THIS BIG...!
I HOPE HE HAS A PERMIT.

ポト
NOW THAT I'M FULL AND IN A GOOD MOOD, I'LL BE EASY ON YOU. ♡
ISN'T THAT RIGHT, ROWEN? ♫
Y-YEAH. EASY.
THAT'S FINE. HERE KITTY, KITTY...! ♡
GAAH!!
WHEN KUEA EATS TOO MUCH, SHE GETS A LITTLE BELLIGERENT.
AAAGH!!
I CAN'T FIGHT THESE GUYS!
I CAME HERE TO SAVE REN!
COU!!

ド
COU--
Oof!
WAIT, PLEASE! YOUR ENEMY CAN USE EDEL RAIDS!
IT'S TOO DANGEROUS WITHOUT US!
HMM...I WONDER HOW IT OPENS...
チラ
THIS COULD BE A PROBLEM.
REN IS ON THE OTHER SIDE OF THIS DOOR.
ARGH!
MOVE ASIDE! I'LL SEE IF MY KEY FITS!

REN!!
C...
OU...

BASTARD!!
WHAT DID YOU DO TO HER?!
COU ...
AND WHO MIGHT YOU BE?
PERCHANCE THE OWNER OF THIS WEAPON?
OH, I MERELY SEARCHED EVERY INCH OF HER.
I WANTED TO SEE WHAT A REAL EDEL RAID IS LIKE.

COU, WAIT!
WHAT DO YOU THINK REN IS?!
WEAPON ...?
OWNER ...?
DON'T RUSH IN UNTIL ROWEN GETS HERE!
YOU CAN'T! HE'S EQUIPPED WITH AN EDEL RAID!
LET GO OF ME!
IF YOU REALLY WANT HER BACK, COME AND GET HER.
WHAT ARE YOU MUTTERING ABOUT, BOY?

RUSHING IN NOW WOULD BE SUICIDE!
CONTROL YOURSELF!
WHAT'S WRONG, BOY?
IK IK
AW...
SAY...
...IS THAT YOUR WEAPON?
COME TO YOUR DOOM.
COME TO BEAZON...

WHAT DID YOU SAY, LITTLE GIRL?!
SIR?
IT'S WEAK.
HUH?!
!!
I WOULDN'T MIND BEING YOUR WEAPON INSTEAD.
?!!!

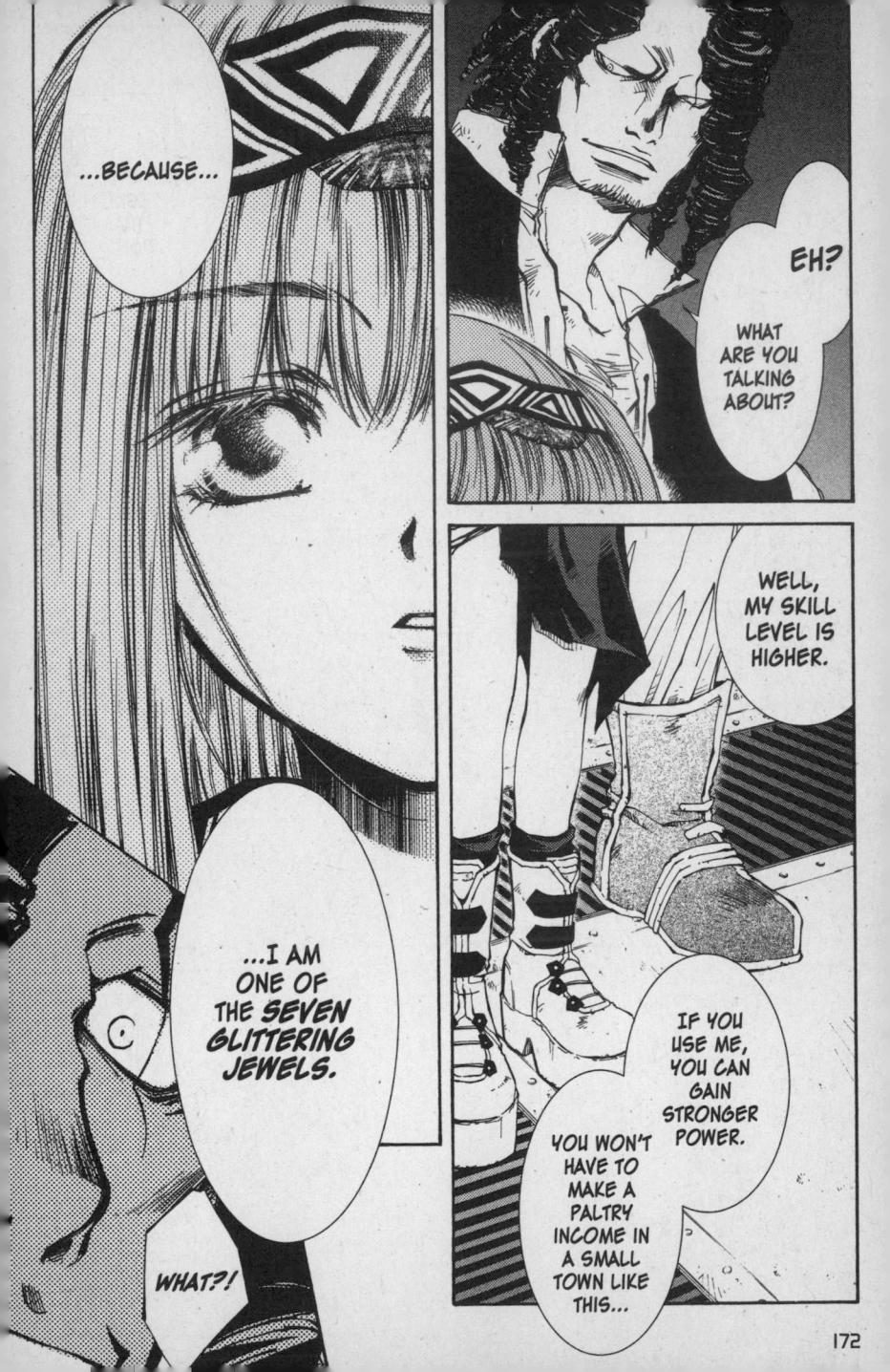
...BECAUSE...
EH?
WHAT ARE YOU TALKING ABOUT?
WELL, MY SKILL LEVEL IS HIGHER.
IF YOU USE ME, YOU CAN GAIN STRONGER POWER.
YOU WON'T HAVE TO MAKE A PALTRY INCOME IN A SMALL TOWN LIKE THIS...
...I AM ONE OF THE SEVEN GLITTERING JEWELS.
WHAT?!

ISN'T THAT RIGHT...
...MISS PROTECTOR?

WHAT ABOUT ME?!
REN... WHAT ARE YOU SAYING?!

THE LAST OF THE METHER-LENCE LINE.
YES. SHE IS ONE OF THE SEVEN GLITTERING JEWELS.

YOU CAN'T USE ME PROPERLY.
I...
I CAN'T ...?
WHY... WHY NOT?
I SHOULD BE WITH SOMEONE WHO WILL USE ME THE MOST EFFICIENTLY.
I AM A WEAPON.

...MAKE ME YOURS.
PLEASE, SIR...
HEH HEH.
AREN'T YOU SWEET?
KYAAAAH!!

Continued in Volume 2

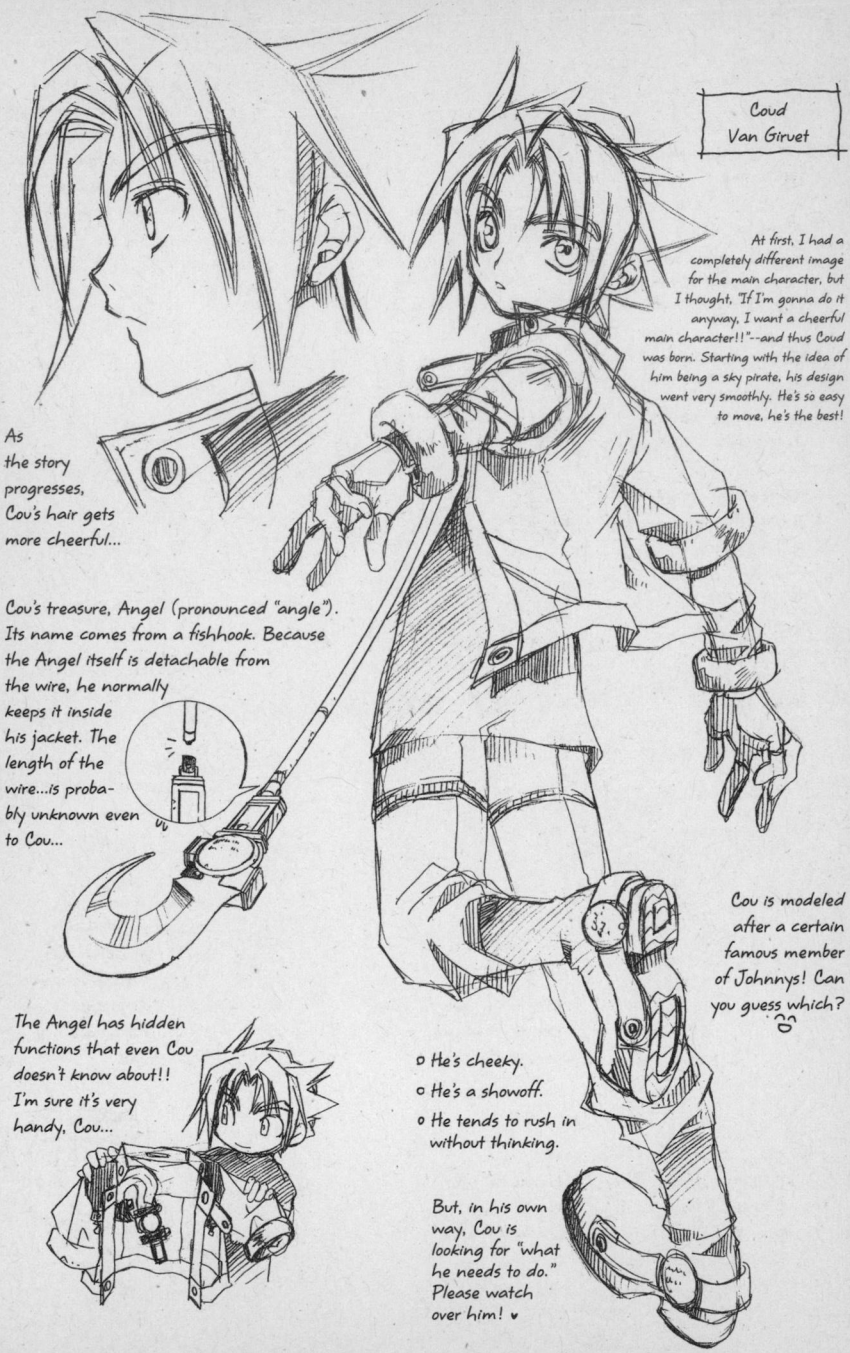
Coud
Van Girvet
At first, I had a completely different image for the main character, but I thought, "If I'm gonna do it anyway, I want a cheerful main character!!"--and thus Coud was born. Starting with the idea of him being a sky pirate, his design went very smoothly. He's so easy to move, he's the best!
As the story progresses, Cou's hair gets more cheerful...
Cou's treasure, Angel (pronounced "angle"). Its name comes from a fishhook. Because the Angel itself is detachable from the wire, he normally keeps it inside his jacket. The length of the wire...is probably unknown even to Cou...
Cou is modeled after a certain famous member of Johnnys! Can you guess which?
The Angel has hidden functions that even Cou doesn't know about!! I'm sure it's very handy, Cou...
He's cheeky.
He's a showoff.
He tends to rush in without thinking.
But, in his own way, Cou is looking for "what he needs to do." Please watch over him!

Reverie
Metherlence

The last member of the Metherlence line, one of the Seven Glittering Jewels said to have power that far surpasses even other Edel Raids.

But, because she had been sealed for so long, she is still only half awake, and adding to that the sleepiness from recharging her Edel Raid power, she is usually very sleepy. She's always dozing off, yawning and bleary-eyed. In that way she's easygoing (laugh).

After reacting, Ren-chan takes the form of a giant sword wrapped in wind. Contrary to her appearance, she is as light as a feather and as sharp and as swift as the wind. It has a color like the malachite color of Ren-chan's Elemental Gelade.

Because it's possible for an Edel Raid to change shape she can change into this giant sword as well.

Ren-chan doesn't really have a model. I was worried about her hair to the very end.

Sleepy version Ren. Ren-chan often has vacant eyes and looks dazed. There is no doubt that Cou will continue to be brandished about by Ren-chan.

Sleepy Ren's goal is to go to "Edel Garden." I think that the reason she is aiming for Edel Garden will become clear as the story progresses. It would be nice if she could learn to get along (?) with everyone by then.

In The Next Volume of

THE SHOWDOWN CONTINUES AS REN OFFERS TO BE BEAZON'S EDEL RAID. HAS SHE GONE TRAITOR? OR DOES SHE HAVE A TRICK OR TWO UP HER SLEEVE? EITHER WAY, COUD AND THE OTHERS WON'T GIVE HER UP WITHOUT A FIGHT! BUT EVEN IF THEY DO DEFEAT BEAZON, THE WORLD IS TEEMING WITH PEOPLE ITCHING TO GET THEIR HANDS ON EDEL RAIDS... A FACT MADE CLEAR WHEN KUEA IS STOLEN BY A EDEL RAID HUNTER NAMED WOLX HOUND. WILL COUD AND THE OTHERS BE ABLE TO RESCUE HER? OR WILL THE HUNTER KEEP HIS PREY?

FIND OUT IN THE NEXT EXCITING VOLUME!

TOKYOPOP®
PRESENTS
FREE
BECK SONG
DOWNLOAD AT
WWW.TOKYOPOP.COM/BECKVSBECK*
BECK
MONGOLIAN CHOP SQUAD™
VS.
Beck
Guerdito
MANGA MASH-UP
FEATURING THE EXCLUSIVE DOWNLOADABLE
SINGLE FROM BECK,
"GO IT ALONE" REMIXED BY SUPERTHRILLER.
INTERSCOPE
RECORDS
*GET YOUR FREE DOWNLOAD
AT WWW.TOKYOPOP.COM/BECKVSBECK
WWW.BECK.COM
© 2006 Harold Sakuishi; © 2005 Interscope Records, Inc.

FOR MORE INFORMATION VISIT: WWW.TOKYOPOP.COM

ARE YOU TRULY ALIVE?

In the collapsing world of the afterlife, two guardians face the ultimate question: Thaddeus yearns for answers, while Mercutio seeks his true love. Will they be able to find it all before it's too late?

ART BY
ROB STEEN
AND STORY BY
STORMCROW HAYES

A MEDITATIVE AND BROODING EXPLORATION INTO THE ENDLESS POSSIBILITIES OF THE AFTERLIFE.

© Sam Hayes, Rob Steen and TOKYOPOP Inc.

READ AN ENTIRE CHAPTER FOR FREE: WWW.TOKYOPOP.COM/MANGAONLINE

• Hoshi no Koe
voices of a distant star™
To what distance would you go for your one true love?
As Mikako travels deeper into space to fight against hostile aliens, her only connection with her boyfriend is through cell-phone text messages. But as the years go by, Mikako barely ages in the timelessness of space while her boyfriend grows old. How can the love of two people, torn apart by war, survive?
Based on Makoto Shinkai's stellar anime!
by Mizu Sahara
ROMANCE
T
TEEN AGE 13+
© M.Shinkai / CW, Mizu Sahara
ART SUBJECT TO CHANGE.

The best of humanity in the worst of wars.

SEIKAI

CREST OF THE STARS™

PRINCESS OF THE EMPIRE

THE NEW MANGA NOVEL SERIES FROM TOKYOPOP

AVAILABLE SEPTEMBER 2006

© 1996 • Hiroyuki Morioka All Rights Reserved • First published in Japan by HAYAKAWA PUBLISHING CORPORATION

CHECK OUT TOKYOPOP'S MANGA NOVELS AT WWW.TOKYOPOP.COM/BOOKS/NOVELS

FOR MORE INFORMATION VISIT: WWW.TOKYOPOP.COM

READ AN ENTIRE CHAPTER FOR FREE: WWW.TOKYOPOP.COM/MANGAONLINE

© YUNA KAGESAKI

CHIBI VAMPIRE VOLUME 2

BY YUNA KAGESAKI

This bloody-good vampire has a big crush on her prey!

Inspired the hit anime!

DEVIL MAY CRY 3 VOLUME 2

BY SUGURO CHAYAMACHI

The secret of the seven seals will release the demon world unto the earth!

It's good against evil... and brother against brother!

© Suguro Chayamachi. © CAPCOM CO., LTD./MEDIA FACTORY, INC.
Devil May Cry™ & © 2006 CAPCOM CO., LTD. All Rights Reserved.

© KEIKO SUENOBU

LIFE VOLUME 2

BY KEIKO SUENOBU

It's about real teenagers...
real high school...
real life!

Every life has a story...
Every story has a life of its own.

READ A CHAPTER ONLINE FOR FREE: WWW.TOKYOPOP.COM/MANGAONLINE

© Svetlana Chmakova and TOKYOPOP Inc.

DRAMACON™

Sometimes even two's a crowd.

When Christie settles in the Artist Alley of her first-ever anime convention, she only sees it as an opportunity to promote the comic she has started with her boyfriend. But conventions are never what you expect, and soon a whirlwind of events sweeps Christie off her feet and changes her life. Who is the mysterious cosplayer who won't even take off his sunglasses indoors? What do you do when you fall in love with a guy who is going to be miles away from you in just a couple of days?

CREATED BY SVETLANA CHMAKOVA!

"YOU CAN'T AVOID FALLING UNDER ITS CHARM." -IGN.COM

READ AN ENTIRE CHAPTER ONLINE FOR FREE:
WWW.TOKYOPOP.COM/MANGAONLINE

STOP!

This is the back of the book. You wouldn't want to spoil a great ending!

This book is printed "manga-style," in the authentic Japanese right-to-left format. Since none of the artwork has been flipped or altered, readers get to experience the story just as the creator intended. You've been asking for it, so TOKYOPOP® delivered: authentic, hot-off-the-press, and far more fun!

DIRECTIONS

If this is your first time reading manga-style, here's a quick guide to help you understand how it works.

It's easy... just start in the top right panel and follow the numbers. Have fun, and look for more 100% authentic manga from TOKYOPOP®!

品質第一公式商品
100%
AUTHENTIC
MANGA